Saint Nicholas

by Regine Schindler and Bro. Kenneth
Illustrated by Carola Schaade

St Paul Publications

It had been a tiring day for young Nick. He had not been to school for he had not quite recovered from a chesty cold. Usually Nick would have enjoyed staying at home with his mum, while Emma, his elder sister and Tim, only a few years older than Nick, had to go to school. But it was Christmas soon and Nick wanted to be around when his teacher was choosing the cast of the end of term play. Nick wanted to be one of the donkeys.

His mother had tried to distract her youngest child but she was so glad when the other two came home from school.

"Do you know what day it is, Nick?" cried Tim as he bounded through the door.

"Course I do," said Nick, "it's Monday."

"December 6th," Emma added.

"Saint Nicholas' Day!" shrieked Tim.

Nick was just about to ask who St Nicholas was when there came three loud bangs on their front door.

"Now who on earth...?" began Dad.

"Why don't they ring the doorbell?" Mum interrupted.

Three more knocks followed louder than before. By this time all the family were a little alarmed. Tim ran to Dad who already had an arm round mum; Emma stood still, looking at the doorway and Nick dived under the table.

"Shall I answer it?" whispered Emma, but her father had left Tim and Mum together, and closing the living-room door was striding towards the front porch. Those who were in the room strained their ears and soon they heard a great guffaw of deep laughter. The door opened and Dad was leading into the room a man dressed from top to toe in a red gown with a hood, trimmed with white wool. On his feet he wore big black boots and he had a huge white beard while he carried in his left hand a long walking-stick and over his shoulder a bulging sack. Within minutes he was sitting down at their table and solemnly shook hands with Emma and Tim.

"You can come out from under there," Tim said to Nick. "It's Father Christmas."

Just as Nick was crawling out from beneath the table, there was a sharp snap and Father Christmas's beard dropped to the floor.

"Uncle Rex," shrieked the children and Nick who was nearest clambered onto Father Christmas's knee.

"You had us scared for a moment, with those heavy knocks," said Dad laughing.

"I wondered if it was you Rex," said Mum as she helped her youngest brother to take off his red cloak and folded it over the back of his chair. "If you're on leave now," she went on, "I take it we won't be seeing you at Christmas?" Rex was in the Navy. He nodded.

"As it was Saint Nicholas' Day, I thought I'd visit my young godson Nick and his sister and brother this evening instead. How do you like my bishop's crook?" He held up his stick for the children to inspect.

"Why a bishop's crook?" said Tim, who was always asking questions.

Emma, the know-all of the family, butted in.

"Saint Nicholas was a bishop, of course."

"OK. But I still don't see the point of Uncle Rex dressing up as Father Christmas but carrying a bishop's crook just because it's Saint Nicholas' Day."

"What is another name for Father Christmas?" broke in Dad before a quarrel began. Tim thought for a moment.

"Santa Claus," he said.

"The Claus is short for Nicholas or Nikolaus in German..." Dad began, "and the..."

"...the Santa means Saint," said Emma. "Father Christmas and Saint Nicholas are the same person!"

"So they are," said Uncle Rex, "and in Northern European countries children are not too sure about meeting him today because although he brings them presents, he also brings a list of their faults through the year and a long stick as well."

"That sounds a very good idea," said Mum, but she was smiling as she spoke.

"Your Christmas presents are in the sack…" The children made a dive towards it but Uncle Rex said, "Not to be opened until Christmas Day. Look I've got a special book about Saint Nicholas. Let's see what it has to say." Nick loved being read to and snuggled up contentedly in his god-father's arms. Tim and Emma too looked at the book while their uncle began the story.

The story of Saint Nicholas has been told and retold for hundreds of years, and each telling, in the days before books were available for everyone, the story was liable to be changed or have bits added, sometimes stories from the life of someone else. The additions were themselves often exaggerated so that nowadays it is hard to sort out fact from fiction. It is so hard that I am not even going to try, but I will tell you the story as I once heard it.

Nicholas was born a long time ago at a town called Patara in the country that we now know as Turkey. His parents were rich and lived in a beautiful house surrounded by a lovely garden. Shortly after his birth, like any other baby, he was given a bath, but unlike most babies he was looked after by maids as well as his loving parents. Imagine the surprise of the whole household when the little baby, only a few hours old, stood up in his first bath. He was obviously going to be a rather special person. As he grew up he might have gone to school, but it is more likely that one of his father's servants became his teacher. He seems to have been an only child, but he got on well with grown-ups. He worked hard at his studies and even enjoyed going to church. In church the stories he liked best were those which he had often heard from his parents, stories about Jesus. Already Nicholas wanted to grow up to be like him.

One Sunday, when he was about fourteen, Nicholas went to church by himself. His parents, who normally would not dream of missing church on Sunday, were both far too unwell to go. As Nicholas returned home, two of the family servants were waiting for him. One look at their faces told Nicholas that something was wrong.

6

"It is much worse than we thought. Your parents are both very ill, you must go to them at once."

Nicholas rushed to his parents' room, threw himself on the floor at their side and looked up anxiously at the family doctor whom the servants had called in. There was little sign of hope in the doctor's eyes and, in a few days, Nicholas was an orphan. How he cried. After the funeral, he shut himself away in his own room for days, barely eating a thing. The servants were very worried about him. What was he doing? Nicholas at first was grieving and feeling very alone. Then he began to think what he ought to do. Although only a boy, he knew he was rich, for the house, the gardens, all the servants (they were probably slaves) and a great deal of gold now belonged to him, but he wanted to be like Jesus, and Jesus certainly had not been born rich.

One day, not so long after the death of his parents, Nicholas had been out for a walk. He was just approaching his own house when he heard some girls crying bitterly. His neighbour, he knew, had three daughters and suddenly Nicholas heard him weeping as well. Nicholas crept up to the wall and listened.

"It's no use," the father was sobbing, "I am so poor I've barely enough money to keep us all in this house. I know you want to be married, my daughter, but where will I find the money to pay for the clothes and all that you will need before any man will marry you? You will have to become a servant and earn your own living."

"I wonder what he is talking about?" thought Nicholas. "His eldest daughter, I expect." But his thoughts were interrupted by more crying as the three girls tried to comfort their father. Nicholas hurried the last few yards to his house, went down his cellar, unlocked a treasure chest, and quickly filled a bag full of gold coins.

That night Nicholas crept back to his neighbour's wall and threw the bag of gold into the house. Luckily, they had left a window wide open. Early next morning while walking in his garden, Nicholas heard his neighbour's cries of joy as the gold was discovered. Now the eldest girl could be married and there was great happiness in their home.

She had only gone away with her new husband six months when

8

Nicholas overheard the second daughter telling a friend that although her father had somehow found the money for her elder sister to be married, there was none left for her and so she would have to leave home and become a servant to earn her own living. That very night a second bag of gold sailed through the open window. The neighbour could hardly believe his eyes and, after his second daughter had left with her husband, he was determined to watch closely to see who was being so kind to his family.

Sure enough, some months later, Nicholas threw a specially large bag of gold through the window. It was so heavy and fell with such a thud that it woke his neighbour up. I wonder why it was so big. Do you think Nicholas was particularly fond of the youngest daughter? Perhaps they had played together when they were children. The noise having woken him up, Nicholas' neighbour leapt out of bed and ran to his window. He could just see the figure of someone hurrying away. The neighbour was over his garden wall in a second and managed to catch Nicholas by the sleeve.

"Are you the one we must thank for giving us all that gold?" Nicholas was flustered. He couldn't actually lie, but on the other hand he didn't want a lot of fuss. By now his neighbour was kneeling in front of him, trying to kiss his hand. Nicholas managed to stop him.

"Please don't tell anyone who helped you," he begged. "It must remain a secret between us."

"That's what Jesus said, when he cured the leper," Uncle Rex said.

"He was growing up like Jesus, wasn't he?" said Emma.

It is possible that when Nicholas eventually left home, he did so having sold up and given all his possessions away so that he might become a monk. Later, for some reason, perhaps he was visiting friends there, Nicholas went to the city of Myra, not so very far from his old home. As he passed through the centre of the town, he made a note of the church so that he could find it next morning when he would be joining the Christians of the city in their prayers.

Next day, when it was still dark, he walked through the silent streets of Myra and found the church just as dawn was beginning to

break. At first, inside the church he could not see a thing and the building appeared quite empty. He always liked to arrive early in a church so that he had time for prayer before the service began. Suddenly he nearly jumped out of his skin. A figure came towards him, an old man who said, "You are to be the new Bishop of Myra. Our old bishop has died and last night I had a dream. In my dream I heard the voice of God who said to me: 'The first man to enter the church as the night is ending shall be your new bishop. His name is Nicholas'. Is your name Nicholas?" and as he spoke, it seemed to Nicholas that the old man could see deep down into his very heart.

"Yes, I'm Nicholas," he stammered, "and I came here to join in morning prayers. I am a servant of Jesus Christ; I want to be like Jesus, but to be a bishop... I couldn't. For one thing, I am far too young and inexperienced."

"Becoming our bishop is how you will serve Jesus," cried another voice. Desperately Nicholas looked round to see who had spoken. By now, daylight was creeping through the windows of the church and Nicholas saw that far from being empty, it was full of people. They had spent the night – he learnt afterwards – the whole night in prayer, waiting for their new bishop.

Without quite realizing what was happening, Nicholas allowed himself to be taken to the Bishop's throne behind the altar. Someone was lighting candles, vestments were being brought from the sacristy, three bishops from neighbouring towns were all ready and by the time the glorious rays of the sun were shining through the church Nicholas, clad in the bishop's cloak and wearing the bishop's hat, was the new Bishop of Myra. How the people of God in that city clapped and cheered!

Soon, stories about the goodness and kindness of Bishop Nicholas of Myra began to spread, not only through the country, but throughout the Roman Empire. Three members of the Imperial Civil Service were present when Nicholas saved the lives of some men wrongfully sentenced to death. Their judge had accepted a bribe to condemn them. Later on, the three Imperial servants found themselves in similar

circumstances and owed their subsequent release to Nicholas. People began to rely on their bishop to help them.

"It's strange," they would say, "he always seems to know when you are in trouble."

People journeyed from miles away just to see him, or to listen to him talking about Jesus and the love of God.

Some sailors when they came ashore got to hear of him; and once, during a terrible storm at sea, a crew battling against high waves were losing control of their ship. They could not steer her and became very frightened. In their terror one of the seamen called out, "Perhaps Nicholas will help us?" His mates had heard of Bishop Nicholas too and so they all cried, "Help us, Nicholas. We are in great need. Please save us."

Suddenly there was another man standing among them; someone they had never seen before. With great strength he caught hold of the tiller and pulled the ropes until the storm had passed. The crew looked at one another in relief, but when they turned to thank the one who had helped them, he was gone.

The sailors agreed that as soon as they docked at Myra, they would all go to church to thank Nicholas for sending help. Secretly, they all believed that the unknown seaman had been an angel. You can imagine their surprise when they saw beneath the beautiful robes of the Bishop of Myra the strong hands and encouraging smile of the one who had saved them from sinking. Down on their knees, they fell in front of Nicholas, but he only replied, "Do please get up. You should be thanking God, not me. I am just his servant and helped you in his name."

"Jesus calmed a storm, didn't he," said Nick.

"He did," said Uncle Rex.

"Nicholas did become more and more like Jesus," murmured Emma, but not too loudly. She was thinking.

You know that in the hotter parts of the world, people sometimes suffer terrible famine. They plant their seed and tend their fields but they only reap a good crop if enough rain falls to water the earth. It so

happened while Nicholas was bishop, that Myra and the land around it suffered a drought for over a year. Nothing grew at all and soon the extra supplies that had been saved from previous plentiful harvests were used up. Naturally the people of the city began to wonder what would happen to them. One day news got around that two ships had docked in the harbour to take on fresh water from the city wells, which hadn't dried up. In the holds and on the decks of these ships were sacks and great jars of wheat. Some hungry citizens ran to Nicholas to tell him what was happening. Breathlessly they explained to him that the seamen had refused to sell any of the food to the city even though there were other ships of the fleet out at sea, waiting for their turn to dock. "They say the food is for the Emperor's court."

Nicholas hurriedly changed his clothes and looking like a merchant, went down to the harbour. He had some money with him and tried to buy some sacks of wheat. The captain of one of the vessels shook his head. "I'm sorry, Sir," he said, "it is out of the question. This corn is destined for the Emperor's household. He'll have me and some of my men flogged if the ship's holds are not full when we arrive at port."

Nicholas looked at the captain, smiled and said, "I promise you, God himself will make up the cargo. The Emperor will be quite satisfied."

The captain could hardly believe his ears. He was just about to tell Nicholas to be off and stop pestering him when he caught the bishop's eye. Of course he didn't know that he was talking to Nicholas. How could this man be so sure that God would help? But there was something about Nicholas that convinced him. Without quite knowing why, he heard himself giving orders that a number of jars and sacks of grain should be carried ashore. At the same time he signalled to the other ships to leave some of their cargo as well.

The food lasted for two years. Nicholas shared it out fairly so that no-one was hungry. There was even enough seed left over to use for the next Spring. And the ships? The people of Myra heard that when they reached the Emperor, they were all quite full.

16

"That's a bit like Jesus feeding the five thousand," said Tim.

Not long before his death, Nicholas received a summons from the Emperor Constantine who had taken it upon himself to call a Council of all the Bishops of the Church to try to settle an argument that was threatening to tear the Church apart. The Council was to meet at Nicea and as the news of their Bishop's journey leaked out in Myra two distracted parents came to seek the help of Nicholas.

Six months earlier they had sent their three sons to school many, many miles from the city. The boys' journey covered the same ground as the bishop would take, and as the poor parents had heard nothing from their sons since they had left, they wondered if Nicholas would make enquiries for the boys on his travels. Their parents had convinced themselves that something dreadful had happened. Each lad had been carrying a bundle of clean clothes together with a wax tablet and stylus for his studies, and gold coins both for the journey and to pay for schooling. Nicholas promised to do what he could, but when he heard about the gold, his heart sank. He had a good idea what had happened to the young scholars. And he was right.

One night, the three had arrived at a wayside inn quite late in the evening. The landlord and his wife agreed to provide a night's lodging, but when they saw how much money the boys had, they decided to take it all. When everyone else was asleep, they stole into the boys' room, killed the lads and took their gold. To hide the bodies was no problem. The landlord cut them up and pickled them in a large wooden brine tub.

Nicholas deliberately went to stay at that inn on his journey to Nicea. He asked the inn-keeper if he had had three boys as guests earlier in the year. Of course the landlord denied it but perhaps he was unable to look Nicholas straight in the eye? Nicholas at any rate, began to wonder.

Just then, a beggar knocked at the door. The inn-keeper's wife opened it and the beggar asked for some food. She looked as though she was going to refuse but the beggar pushed her aside. "I'm hungry!" he cried, and strode towards the wooden barrel which stood in the

corner of the room. When he took off the lid, he began to shout, "There's a boy's arm here. Help! Help! Murder!" and he rushed out of the inn. Nicholas went to the barrel, made a sign of the cross over it and found himself helping three boys, all fit and well, to clamber out.

"What happened to the landlord and his wife?" demanded Emma.

"I'm not quite sure," said Uncle Rex. "I daresay Nicholas helped them to be sorry for what they had done. He always liked that to happen. But you can see why Nicholas has become a Patron Saint of children."

"When did he return to Myra?" said Tim.

"It looks as though he died before the Council of Nicea which began in the year 325 AD. In later times school children in many towns throughout Europe celebrated a Saint Nicholas' feast not long before Christmas. One boy was chosen to play Nicholas and was dressed up as a bishop. He could give all the orders for one day. The grown-ups dressed up too, and they put on masks, pretending to be devils or animals. They would put on thick furs and make a lot of noise. 'We are driving out Winter,' they shouted. It was often very wild and rowdy. 'This is a fools' feast – it should be forbidden,' some clergymen thought, but the children enjoyed it, especially the procession.

The main character in the procession was always Saint Nicholas. You could recognise him by his mitre, his bishop's hat," said Uncle Rex. "Look, he has someone with him, his servant Rupert. It is Rupert who wore a red cloak and hood. He was the one who used to ask the children if they had been good and said their prayers. Nicholas himself was always very friendly and gave out presents."

"So, strictly speaking," said Emma, "Father Christmas ought to be dressed as a bishop. That's why you brought a bishop's crook with you."

"You've got it," said Uncle Rex.

"Saint Nicholas is much more exciting than Father Christmas," said Tim, "and Dad would look good dressed up as a devil. Aren't there a few churches who have revived the custom of appointing a Boy-Bishop? Perhaps we should do it at our church."

20

"I want to be the Boy-Bishop," said Nick.

"You're too young," snapped Tim.

"Don't squabble," said Uncle Rex. "You should remember how much Nicholas wanted to be like Jesus." Their faces fell. "Help me back into my gown and beard. I'm going to visit your cousins now. Would you like this book about your saint, Nicky?"

"Yes, please, Uncle Rex." Nick ran to show his mother the book.

"Will I be well enough to go to school tomorrow?" he pleaded. "I want to show them who Father Christmas really is."

Notes for parents and teachers

There is little or no evidence for any of the stories about St Nicholas. All that we can be certain of is that he was Bishop of Myra and that he either attended or at least responded to the summons to attend the Council of Nicea in 325 AD when the views of the arch-heretic Arius were refuted by that Ecumenical Council. Such stories that we have are to be found in the Golden Legend of mediaeval times.

He is Patron Saint not only of children, but also of sailors, of pawnbrokers, whose symbol of three golden balls outside their premises are said to be representations of the three dowries.

In his guise as Father Christmas he still plays an important part in the lives of small children. They "believe in him" for varying lengths of time, and the good natured conspiracy between parents and older siblings can be a source of great fun, while at the same time providing horrid opportunities for spiteful brothers to destroy the mystery by disclosing who it is who really fills the stocking at the end of the bed.

This book might help reveal the truth in a manner that is not totally destructive. By taking off his costume Uncle Rex is making the point while at the same time introducing the reader to St Nicholas.

Although the prefix St is not used a great deal the real meaning of the word is referred to throughout the text, for is not a Saint a reflection of Jesus Christ? "It is no longer I who live, but Christ who lives in me." (Gal 2:20). The parallels between the life of Jesus and the stories of Nicholas are quite deliberate. Similarly the reader can go on discovering ways in which the Saint reflects Jesus. He provides help when needed; he does not want to be repaid.

The gifts that he gave the girls were just what they needed when they needed them, and our own present giving is far better if it actually responds to a particular need. In other words Nicholas encourages us to take immense care in choosing gifts for others. The stories of St Nicholas could well become suitable material for Advent, and provide yet another opportunity for parents and guardians to retell the stories of Jesus, his care for others, especially the poor and outcast.

St Nicholas has always been a popular saint. The appointment of Boy-Bishops where it happens is almost certainly a revival which probably goes back further than this century. Ancient parish churches in ports are frequently dedicated to him, as you might expect, but his appearance as Father Christmas probably goes back not much more than a hundred and fifty years.

The language in which this story has been written is fairly easy so that a child who can read reasonably well will be able to manage it alone. When you come to words that the child cannot manage DO NOT turn what is an enjoyable experience into a reading exercise. Give the child the word immediately, with care you can even anticipate which words might be a problem, such as "shrieked" or "guffaw" on page 2, "Northern European"on page 4 and so on.

Original title: *Sankt Nikolaus* © 1989 Verlag Ernst Kaufmann, Lahr, W. Germany
Translated from the German and adapted for English by Anne Richards and Bro. Kenneth

St Paul Publications
Middlegreen, Slough SL3 6BT, England

English translation copyright © St Paul Publications 1990
ISBN 085439 335 8
Printed by MacLehose & Partners Ltd, Portsmouth

St Paul Publications is an activity of the priests and brothers of the Society of St Paul
and the Daughters of St Paul who proclaim the Gospel through the media of social communication

USING MAPS

Our environment

by Susan Hoe

ticktock

By Susan Hoe
Series consultant: Debra Voege
Editor: Mark Sachner
Project manager: Joe Harris
***ticktock* designer: Hayley Terry**
Picture research: Lizzie Knowles and Joe Harris

Copyright © 2008 ticktock Entertainment Ltd.
First published in Great Britain by ticktock Media Ltd.,
Unit 2, Orchard Business Centre, North Farm Road, Tunbridge Wells, Kent TN2 3XF, Great Britain.

A CIP catalogue record for this book is available from the British Library.

ISBN 978 1 84696 725 2

Printed in China

PICTURE CREDITS

China Images/ Alamy: 17tl. Victor Englebert/ photographersdirect.com: 20t, 21t. Getmapping PLC: 24c. Sean Harris: 4b, 8. iStock: 4t, 6t, 7b, 11tr, 11c, 12t, 12b, 19tl, 22t, 25b. Jupiter Images: 2. Lehtikuva Oy/ Rex Features: 19tr. Oliver Polet/ Corbis: 17b. Ulli Seer/ Getty Images: 5t. Shutterstock: 6b, 11tl, 11b, 15bl, 15br, 17tr, 18b, 19b, 24tl, 24b, 25t, 25c. Justin Spain: 4c, 9 all, 21b, 31t. Hayley Terry: 5b, 10, 13 all, 15t, 19c, 27, 30. Tim Thirlaway: 28, 29. Time and Life Pictures/ Getty Images: 20b. www.mapart.co.uk: 7t, 14, 16, 18, 22b, 23, 26, 31b.

Contents

Words in **bold** are explained in the glossary.

What is a map?

A map is a special drawing. This drawing is usually of an area as seen from above.

This area can be as big as the world. Or it can be as small as a classroom in your school!

Making a map of an island

Map Key

 Trees/woods

 Roads/footpaths

 Grey-roofed buildings

 Red-roofed buildings

 Piers

Gardens

Maps help us find things as if we were directly above them.

In this book, we will learn about some ways that maps tell us about the environment. But first let's look at some of the ways that maps help us.

Find the biggest building in the photo of the island.

Now find it on the map.

Why do we need maps?

Maps help us find our way around. They give us all kinds of information about where we live.

A map can help you get from one place to another. It can show you where you are, where you want to go, and how to get there.

Weather map of the UK and Ireland

This map shows you what the weather will be like where you live.

Can you tell what kinds of weather this map is showing?

Map of the world

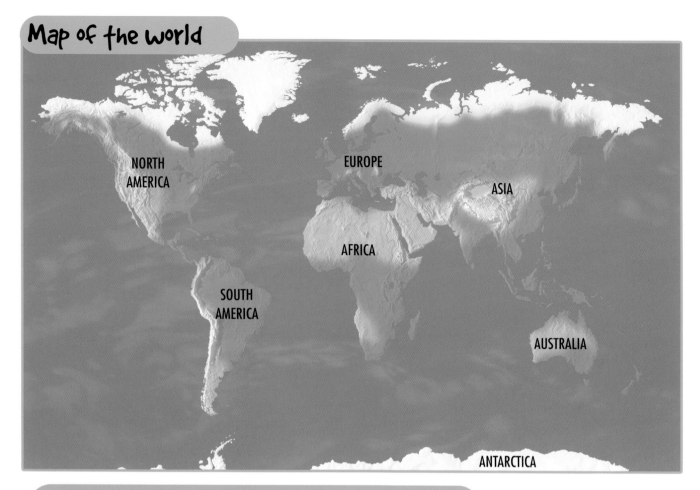

NORTH AMERICA

EUROPE

ASIA

AFRICA

SOUTH AMERICA

AUSTRALIA

ANTARCTICA

This map shows the world's deserts in yellow. The forests and woods are in green. Places covered in snow and ice are white.

Maps teach us important facts about places. These places might be close to home or on the other side of the world.

Maps show us whether the land is flat or hilly. They can show us where people and animals live. We can also learn what crops are grown and what sorts of things are made in a place.

Maps are handy and easy to use. They can show us huge areas in a small amount of space. We can take them just about anywhere!

Mapping your Classroom

Maps show how a place seems if you are looking down on it. That place can be your country or your town. It can even be a classroom in your school!

A 3-D classroom

This classroom is a **three-dimensional (3-D)** space. The room and things in the room are solid. They have length, width, and **depth**.

A 2-D map

A map is a **two-dimensional (2-D)** drawing of a space. Everything in the classroom now looks flat.

To create a 2-D map of this classroom, we draw all the flat shapes on a piece of paper.

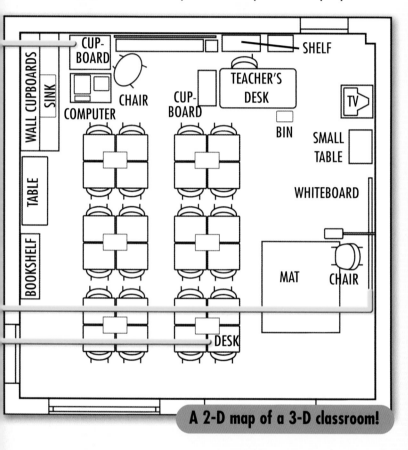

WALL CUPBOARDS
SINK
CUP-BOARD
COMPUTER
CHAIR
CUP-BOARD
SHELF
TEACHER'S DESK
TV
BIN
SMALL TABLE
WHITEBOARD
TABLE
BOOKSHELF
MAT
CHAIR
DESK

A 2-D map of a 3-D classroom!

This map shows you how to find everything in the classroom.

Find the teacher's desk.

Find the shelves.

Making the map

This drawing of the classroom was made from the photograph.

Pretend you are able to float up above the room and look down on it.

When you are right above the room, it looks flat. This is the view we use to make a 2-D map.

Mapping a place for a new school

*A new school needs lots of land to be built on. It must have a school building, car park, and playground. To run smoothly, the school needs special **services** from the town.*

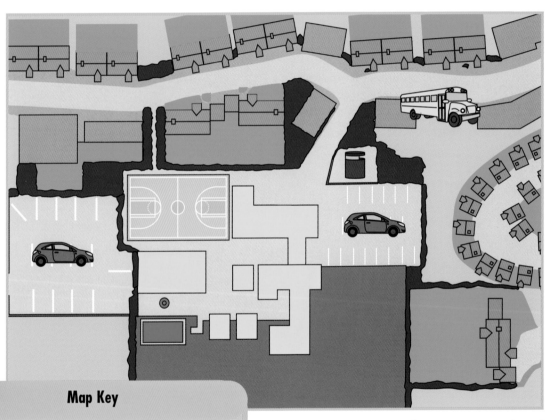

Map Key

🚗	Car park	⬜	Shops
🏀	Playground	◎	Water fountain
🚌	Bus stop	⬛	Hedge
🗑	Rubbish bins	⬜	Gardens
⬜	School building	⬜	School playing field
🏠	Residential homes	⬜	Swimming pool

This map shows what a new school needs. It uses different symbols to identify each thing. The map has a key. This **map key** is also called a legend. It tells you what each symbol stands for.

Find the playground.

Find the bus stop.

10

Town services

Towns provide many services that schools need.

The electrical plant supplies all the electricity.

A town **reservoir** holds the water used in the school. This reservoir is formed by a large **dam**.

New roads are built so that students can get to school.

The rubbish is taken to the city dump. Some items are taken to a **recycling** plant.

Changes in your town's environment

When a new building goes up, it causes changes in the area.

A new school can mean more classrooms and better student equipment.

A new school can also cause traffic jams, however. More traffic can mean more air **pollution** from cars.

Making good choices for the environment

The town of Summerton needs a new hospital. You must decide where to build it. Look at this map of Summerton and the two hospital plans. Which plan would you choose? Which one would be better for the town's **environment** and harm fewer fields, forests and lakes? Why?

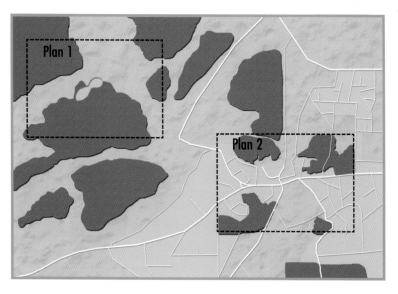

Map Key

- Field
- Forest
- Lake
- Road
- Town
- Proposed site

Plan 1

The hospital will be built in a wooded area far from town. There are no roads around. Trees must be cut down and the pond emptied and filled in with soil to make more building space. A cement car park will be built.

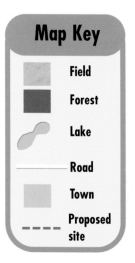

Plan 2

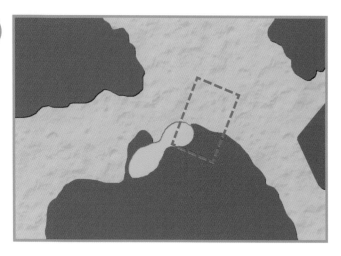

The hospital will be built in a field that is near a main road. More trees will be planted around the building. A car park will be built under the ground. It will not be seen from the road.

Changes in our country's environment

*You can show more than just the streets of your home town on a map. In fact you can show the roads of a whole country! Roads let people and **goods** move across the United Kingdom.*

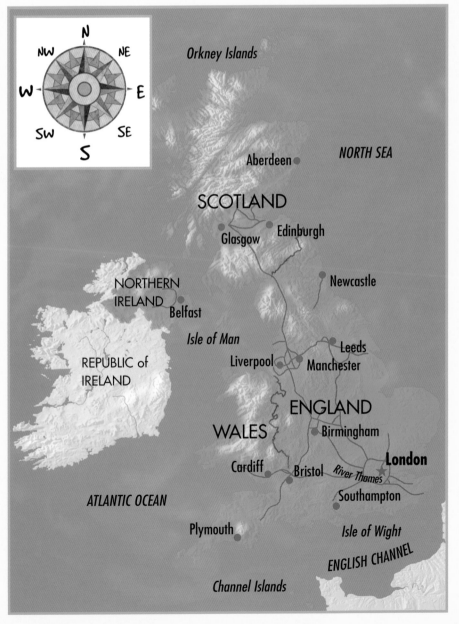

This map shows the most important roads in the United Kingdom, called motorways. They go through cities, fields, mountains, coastal areas, and even over waterways. Some go east and west. Some travel north to south. Many cross over each other.

The **compass rose** at the top left of this map shows you which direction is north (N), south (S), east (E), or west (W). It may also show northeast (NE), southeast (SE), southwest (SW), and northwest (NW).

Over many years, people have built roads, bridges, airports, and railways across the United Kingdom.

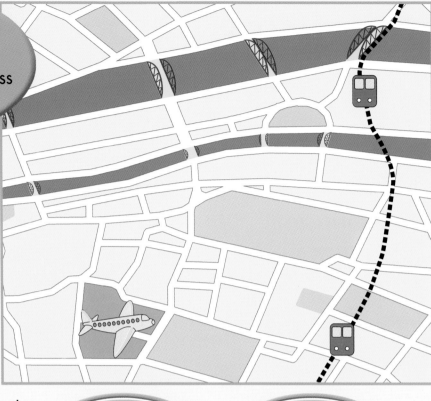

Map Key

Bridge

Railway track

Airport

Road

River

Parkland

This city map shows many roads and man-made **structures**.

Find a bridge.

Find the railway track.

on the road

Clean roads and motorways help us to protect the environment. They also protect the natural beauty of an area.

Roads take people to their destinations. Be kind to the environment when travelling by car.

Travel with litter bags to store your rubbish. Empty them when you have reached your destination.

Where do people live around the world?

Most people gather where there is water and food. They also want safe roads and ways to get to shops and other locations. When many people live in a place, they make a big impact on their environment.

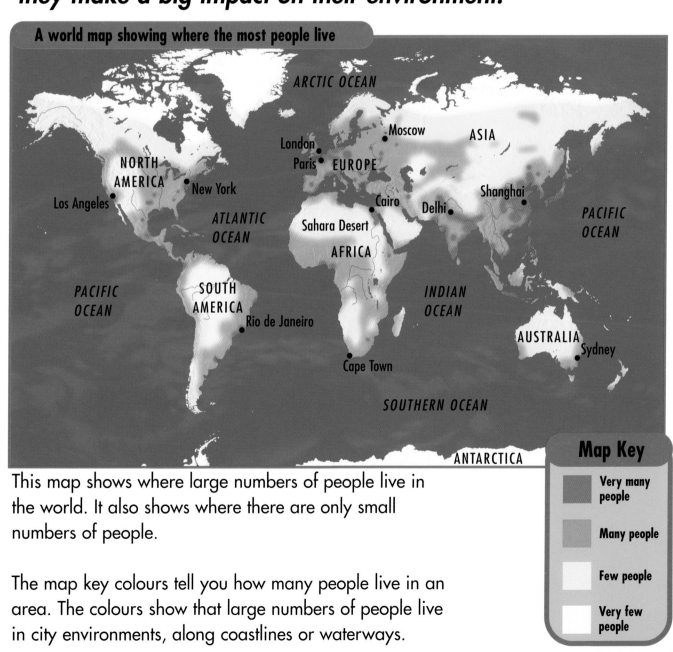

A world map showing where the most people live

ARCTIC OCEAN

Moscow

ASIA

London
Paris
EUROPE

NORTH
AMERICA
New York

Los Angeles

ATLANTIC
OCEAN

Cairo

Delhi

Shanghai

PACIFIC
OCEAN

Sahara Desert

AFRICA

PACIFIC
OCEAN

SOUTH
AMERICA
Rio de Janeiro

INDIAN
OCEAN

AUSTRALIA
Sydney

Cape Town

SOUTHERN OCEAN

ANTARCTICA

Map Key

Very many people

Many people

Few people

Very few people

This map shows where large numbers of people live in the world. It also shows where there are only small numbers of people.

The map key colours tell you how many people live in an area. The colours show that large numbers of people live in city environments, along coastlines or waterways.

The Sahara Desert in Africa has very little natural water. Therefore, very few people live there.

Shanghai is a city in China. It has a big seaport. For humans, it is one of the most crowded environments in the world.

Fighting pollution

People are the cause of most pollution in the world. But people also help solve many pollution problems. **Governments** and groups like **UNICEF** are working to clean up the environment.

The new well in this African village has been built by UNICEF.

A rainforest environment

Rainforests are areas of land with thick plant growth. Millions of animals live there, too. Some living things in Earth's rainforests are still waiting to be discovered!

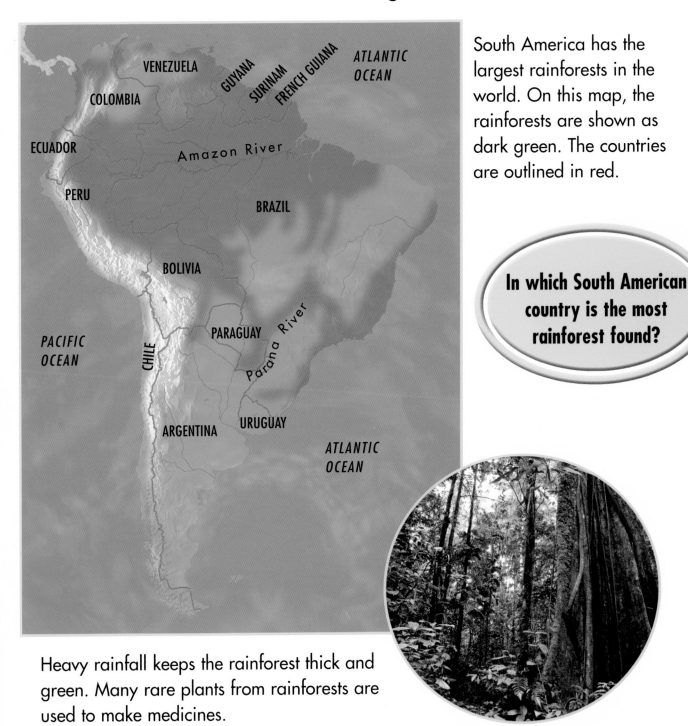

South America has the largest rainforests in the world. On this map, the rainforests are shown as dark green. The countries are outlined in red.

VENEZUELA
GUYANA
SURINAM
FRENCH GUIANA
ATLANTIC OCEAN
COLOMBIA
ECUADOR
Amazon River
PERU
BRAZIL
BOLIVIA
PACIFIC OCEAN
CHILE
PARAGUAY
Parana River
ARGENTINA
URUGUAY
ATLANTIC OCEAN

In which South American country is the most rainforest found?

Heavy rainfall keeps the rainforest thick and green. Many rare plants from rainforests are used to make medicines.

The rainforests are shrinking.
Too many trees are being cut down.
This process is called 'deforestation'.

The harpy eagle is in danger of becoming **extinct**.

When so many trees are cut down, many rainforest animals lose their homes and die out.

Deforestation of a rainforest area

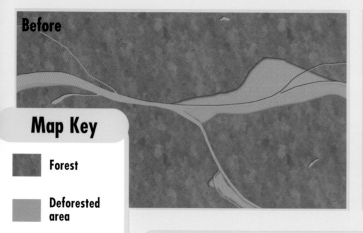

Before

After

Map Key

Forest

Deforested area

River

These 'before' and 'after' maps show how much of this rainforest has disappeared.

How can you help?

Paper is made from wood. Try to recycle paper so fewer trees are cut down to make new paper. When you buy paper, look for the symbol on the right. It means the paper is recycled.

People are working to save rainforests and the animals that live there.

Mapping a rainforest village

The rainforest of Brazil is home to different groups of people. One such group is the Yanomami tribe.

This is Shoco, a young Yanomami boy. He and his family live with other families not far from a river. Their way of life is in danger from deforestation.

The Yanomamis eat fish that they catch from their canoes on the river. They also eat meat from the animals they hunt in the rainforest.

Shoco and his family sleep in hammocks that are hung inside their house.

The tribe gathers nuts
and fruits in the rainforest.
They also grow sweet potatoes
and plantains (a type of banana) in
their gardens.

The Yanomamis live all
together in a large
doughnut-shaped house
called a shabono.

This map of a Yanomami home uses symbols that stand
for different parts of the house. The map key helps you
understand what the symbols mean.

Map of Shoco's home

Map Key

⬮	Hammock
✳	Fireplace
▥	Shelving
●	Post
✺	Tall tree
▦	Roof
▦	Rainforest

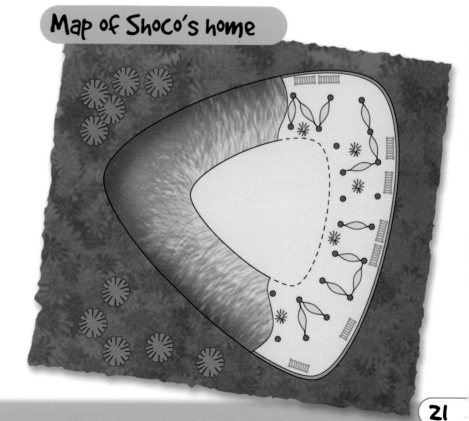

Drawing maps

Before you can draw a map, you must figure out the exact size and shape of the mapping area. This means figuring out how to measure large areas.

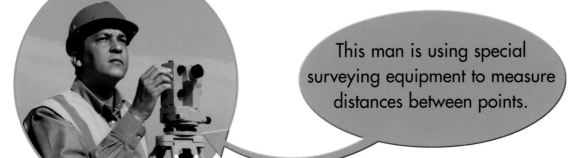

This man is using special surveying equipment to measure distances between points.

Mapmakers use their measurements to draw their maps. The maps on these pages show the attractions at an amusement park.

Scale: shrinking to fit

When mapmakers have gathered all their measurements, they must figure out how to fit them onto a piece of paper. So they shrink, or scale down, the real measurements to make a map.

0   15 metres

This small-scaled map shows a fairly large area. Many objects are visible, but they are quite small.

Different scales used to map the same area change what you see. Small-scale maps show large areas on a sheet of paper. Large-scale maps show smaller areas, but the objects look bigger and have more detail.

The map **scale** tells you how long a metre is on the map. This way you can figure out real distances on the map.

0   8 metres

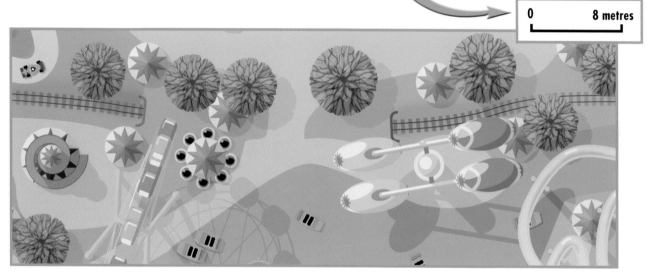

This larger-scaled map shows a smaller area than the first map. The map scale also shows that each centimetre is equal to fewer metres. So you see fewer objects on this map, but you can see them in greater detail.

0   5 metres

This map has the largest scale. It shows an even smaller area. You see even fewer objects, but you can see them in even greater detail.

Hi-tech mapmaking

Many years ago, people used their travels to figure out the shape of the land. Today, mapmakers use new, hi-tech equipment.

Mapmakers can take many photographs of the ground from a plane.

This photograph shows the ground below as seen from the plane.

The pictures and measurements taken from the plane are sent to computers that draw a map.

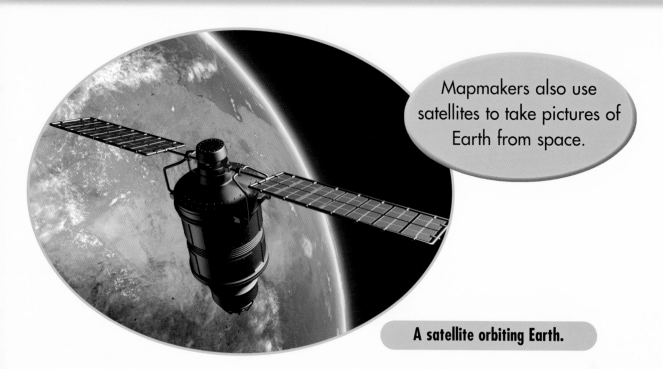

Mapmakers also use satellites to take pictures of Earth from space.

A satellite orbiting Earth.

The pictures taken by these satellites are beamed back to Earth. They are put together to make pictures of our planet, like the one shown here. These pictures can then be turned into maps.

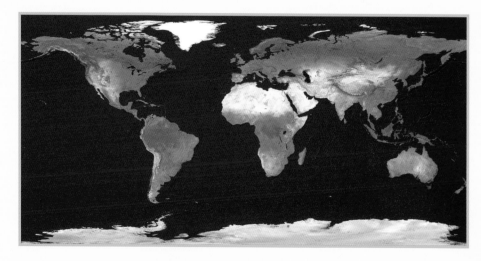

Ever-changing maps

Satellites can tell where your car is on the road. They can produce road maps that help you find your destination. These maps constantly change as you need them. The maps are called GPS, or Global Positioning System, maps.

A GPS map at work in a car.

Mapping natural disasters in South America

Natural disasters are sudden events like earthquakes or hurricanes, which cause great damage to a place.

- Volcanic eruption 1985
- Hurricane 1968, 1996
- Hurricane 1968, 1996
- Earthquake 1949
- Earthquake 1970
- Wildfire 1998
- Earthquake 2007
- Tsunami 1868, 1960
- Hurricane 2004
- Earthquake 1939
- Tornado 1973
- Earthquake 1944

South America has had many natural disasters. Here's a way to map out these events from the past.

Making a map of natural disasters

1. Copy the map of South America on page 26 onto a blank sheet of paper. You could also use a thin piece of tracing paper to trace the map.

2. Now make a map key. Draw symbols on it to represent earthquakes, volcanic eruptions, tsunamis, hurricanes, tornadoes and wildfires.

3. The map on page 26 shows where each of these natural disasters happened. Use this map key as a guide to draw your own natural disaster pictures on your map of South America. Be sure to draw the natural disaster symbols so they look like the ones in your map key.

Map Key

Earthquake: a strong shaking of the ground.

Volcanic eruptions: when hot lava from inside the earth bursts out of a volcano.

Tsunami (tidal wave): a destructive giant wave, caused by an earthquake under the ocean.

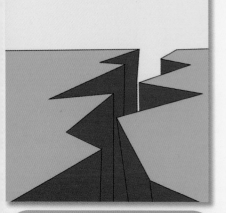

Tornado: a funnel-shaped wind that can pick up heavy objects.

Wildfire: a very bad fire that spreads quickly through forested areas.

Hurricane: a strong storm with high winds and heavy rains.

Making a map of your own beach

A beach is a fun natural environment to visit. Why not make your own beach map? Make a map key too so your friends can find all the great things in it.

What kind of shape will your beach be? Circle, oval, crescent, rectangle?

How many lifeguard stations will it have? Where will they be placed?

Alex's Amazing Beach

What fun things can people do at your beach? Will there be a pier for fishing, paddleboats, an ice cream stall, or a crazy golf course?

Does your beach have public toilets, outdoor showers, a car park, or a first aid station?

Step 1

Draw the shape of your beach on a piece of paper. Is it on an ocean or a lakefront?

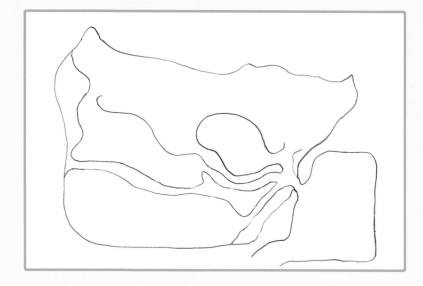

Step 2

Make up different symbols for all the beach items you want to include on your map. Be sure you leave enough space between all the different symbols. Draw in the sandy beach area, any grassy areas, and car parks.

Step 3

Colour your beach map, and give the beach a name.

Step 4

Make your map key using the symbols on your map.

Water	Shower	Food stall	Crazy golf
Pier	Sand	Public toilets	Parking
Lifeguard tower	Water fountain	First aid	Rowing boats hire
Grass	Rubbish bin	Picnic area	Play area

Glossary

Compass rose: a drawing that shows directions on a map: north (N), south (S), east (E) and west (W).

Dam: a concrete wall that holds back water.

Depth: the length from the top of a space or an object to its bottom.

Environment: the area and space where people, plants, and animals live.

Equipment: tools and other items used for a specific job.

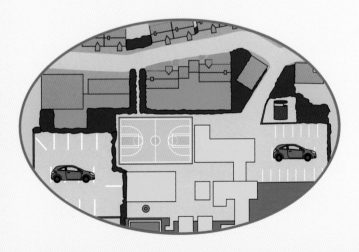

Extinct: when a kind of animal has died out, and none are alive any more.

Goods: items that people grow or make. People can buy and sell goods.

Governments: the groups of people who make the laws and rule in a country or area.

Map key: the space on a map that shows the meaning of any pictures or colours used on the map.

Pollution: unclean things found in the air, soil, and water.

Rainforests: large wooded areas with lots of warm rainfall that produce big trees and shrubs. Little sunlight gets through the thick growth of trees.

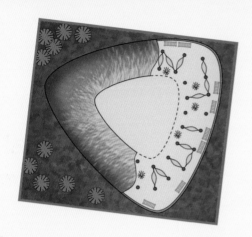

Recycling: turning rubbish into something that can be used again – especially cans, glass, plastic, and paper.

Reservoir: a place where fresh water is collected and stored for people to use.

Scale: the amount by which the measurement of an area is shrunk to fit on a map. The map scale is a drawing or symbol that tells how to measure distances on a map.

Services: needed and useful help offered to people living in an area. Some services are rubbish disposal, recycling, water, and electricity.

Structures: buildings and other large man-made objects.

Three-dimensional (3-D): appearing as a solid thing that has length, width, and depth.

Two-dimensional (2-D): appearing as a flat shape with only length and width.

UNICEF: United Nations International Children's Emergency Fund (now called simply United Nations Children's Fund); a group that helps keep children healthy and safe.

Index